TOLPUDDLE
BOY

Transported to hell and back

Alan Brown

ited

The author gives grateful thanks to Janet Pickering of the Tolpuddle Martyrs Museum in Tolpuddle, Dorset, and to Christine Coates of the TUC Library Collections, University of North London, for their help in researching this book.

The 'hell' of the title refers specifically to a convict's life in the penal colonies of Australia, in the nineteenth century.

Text copyright 2002 © Alan Brown
Published by Hodder Children's Books 2002

Picture 1   Used by kind permission of the TUC
Picture 2   Political Drama No 32 (H044/27), Public Record Office
Picture 3   Used by kind permission of the TUC
Picture 4   © Sue Wilson 2000

The drawing of the Tolpuddle Martyrs beneath the sycamore tree in Tolpuddle on the title page and chapter headings in this book is the copyright of the TUC, and is used by their kind permission. The 'Wages of Despair' budget on page 31 is the property of the TUC, and is used by their kind permission.

Book design by Jane Hawkins
Cover illustration by Stuart Haygarth
Map by Tony Fleetwood

The right of Alan Brown to be identified as the author of the work has been asserted by him in accordance with the Copyright, Designs and Patents Act 1988.

10 9 8 7 6 5 4 3 2 1

A catalogue record for this book is available from the British Library.

ISBN: 0 340 852038

Printed by Bookmarque Ltd, Croydon, Surrey

Hodder Children's Books
a division of Hodder Headline Limited
338 Euston Road
London NW1 3BH

J

1305819

Contents

To the memory of James Brine
1813–1902

Foreword

Imagine you are on a little wooden ship, tossed by a stormy sea. Your legs are chained to the timbers of one of the lowest and darkest holds. The hatches are shut and there is no light and little air. There is not enough space to lie down and you sit with your head in your hands, horribly seasick. When your stomach heaves up the bread and foul water you ate many hours ago, you can only turn your head to one side and spew on to the floor.

You wear filthy rags. If you ask the guard for a drink, he beats you with a heavy stick and nearly breaks your bones.

Around you are dozens of other wretches, mostly ill and sick. Toilet buckets are overflowing, and the smell is appalling. All around there is wailing and moaning, cursing and swearing. The ship pitches and wallows. The timbers creak and groan. You think you are going to die. You think you are already in hell.

It is 1834, and you are a convict, being transported to Australia. There are hundreds aboard this ship, kept from mutiny by shackles and brutal floggings with the dreaded cat-o'-nine tails. Conditions are so bad, many prisoners never reach Sydney. The dead are pitched overboard with no ceremony. Sharks follow the trail of bodies, gorging on corpses. Will one of them be yours?

You are hardly more than a boy, with a sweetheart back in England. You have committed no crime, and should have the best of your life before you. It takes all your courage not to fall into deepest despair.

Why are you in such an awful place?

All this, and more, really happened to a boy named James Brine. His story is one of love and hope, danger and suffering, courage and determination. There are heroes and heroines, spies and villains, and hazardous journeys from one side of the world to the other. Follow James now on his adventures.

James Brine

J AMES Brine's stomach growls with hunger. His last meal was a thin stew of potatoes and turnips, yesterday. His scratchy wool shirt and britches hang loosely on his thin body and his feet are bare in the dirt of Tolpuddle's main street. He is pale-skinned, but with the dark hair of Dorset.

He squeezes between the men standing in the crowd. They turn in anger at his pushing, but when they see that he is just a boy they let him through. They hope to find work this morning, but James is no competition!

Now he can see his father, John, dressed like the other labourers in coarse cloth smock, baggy trousers and hobnailed boots. John Brine has a good place on the edge of the village green.

The farmers arrive on horseback. Their frockcoats are of fine cloth and their riding boots of soft leather. They are wealthy men, come to hire labourers and make themselves wealthier through other men's work.

The lord of the manor's steward also arrives, to hire for the manor farm. His lordship does not live in Tolpuddle, but he owns most of it. Even the farmers pay him rent for their land and grand houses.

The labourers take off their caps in respect to all these fine gentlemen. James struggles to see and hear. Will his father be hired? If he is, there will be food tonight!

The farmers and the lord's steward do not want many men. The corn has been planted and the harvest is months away. There are only animals to tend, walls and hedges to be repaired. They do not bother to get down from their glossy horses, but simply point at the labourers they want.

A finger points at James's father.

John Brine grins. He asks his wage and is told, 'One shilling for an honest day's work.' His grin fades. A loaf of bread costs more than that!

'Take it or leave it!' growls the farmer.

Every farmer offers the same, and his lordship is a farmer when it comes to hiring men. They have agreed amongst themselves to keep wages lower in Tolpuddle than anywhere else in Dorset.

James's father puts on his cap and trudges off to work. Today he was lucky. Tomorrow he might not be chosen at all.

A popular song of the time called 'Eight Shillings A Week' describes the plight of the poor in the countryside. Eight shillings (about £10 in today's money) might feed a single man, but there were often six or more children in a family in those days.

Our venerable fathers remember the year,
When a man earned three shillings a day
  and his beer,
He then could live well, keep his family neat,
But now he must work for Eight Shillings a
  week.

A poor man to labour (believe me 'tis so)
To maintain his family is willing to go
Either hedging or ditching, to plough or to
*   reap,*
But how does he live on Eight Shillings a
*   week?*

As a child, James Brine was always hungry. He and the rest of his family lived – just – on stews made from root vegetables. Sometimes, they might have a little bread. They could not afford meat.

Yet James was born in 1813 in the heart of the countryside! Wheat was growing in the fields and there were lots of small game animals, like rabbits and pheasants, that were good to eat. To understand this poverty in the midst of plenty, we will follow James away from the hiring place on the village green.

This is the main road from nearby Dorchester to London, many miles away. Several times a week, a stagecoach rattles by on the two-day journey to the capital. Yet the road is just a dusty track.

To left and right are small cottages, some stone and thatched with reeds, others brick with tiled roofs. Some have only one room, with a family living at one end, animals at the other.

The houses are owned by the farmers, and the lord of the manor. If a labourer complains about his pay, his family can be turned out on the street.

Children are playing barefoot in that street. James greets them. He knows everybody, for there are only ten children of his age living in Tolpuddle. There are about one hundred children below the age of ten, and about 350 people of all ages in the village.

The children are not at school, because there isn't one. Very few poor people can read or write. If they have to sign their names, someone else does it for them and then they add their 'mark', a shaky cross scratched with a quill pen.

We walk past the church, the grandest building James has ever entered. His family worship there every Sunday. James is afraid of the vicar, who he thinks is the cleverest man in the village.

The vicarage is a big house, in gardens set back from the road. It is described in church records of the time as having '5 small bed chambers, one [large] room below stairs – a parlour, a kitchen and a sitting room, a pantry, brewhouse, dairy and cellar'.

The vicar is lucky, compared to the labourers! It is easy to understand why he seems to side with the land and property owning gentry. In fact, many churchmen are also rich landowners themselves.

The church in Tolpuddle is next to the manor house. The lord of the manor paid for the place of worship to be built, and choses a vicar who will do what he is told.

If we follow James all round the village we pass the Rose and Crown public house, and several smaller alehouses. We see smoke and steam rise from the smithy and hear the clanging of iron on iron. The wheel on the water mill is constantly turning as it grinds corn for the village. The miller is another wealthy man. Villagers are not allowed to take their corn to anyone else, however much he charges.

The farmers live further away from the village, in farmsteads rather unimaginatively called East,

West and Middle Farms. On the fringe of the parish is another manor house, Southover. A notice of sale in 1828 said that '...The farms are in a high state of cultivation. Game is plentiful, and the River affords good Trout fishing.'

This is just sport for the gentry. Laws have made all game animals the property of the few rich people who own all the land. If poor folk kill rabbits or deer they are arrested and punished for poaching. They might even be shot by one of the dangerous spring-guns set by gamekeepers to trap the unwary.

Other laws have taken the common land away from villages. So labourers cannot graze their own animals, or grow their own food. They are worse off, according to at least one visitor to England, than the slaves in America. No wonder James is always hungry!

We pass the old Kings Arms inn, now a workhouse. It reminds us that families who cannot feed themselves are split up and made to work long hours for their keep. We see two women carrying washing across the yard. On their right shoulders they wear a large letter P, telling everyone that they live on the charity of the parish. It is a shameful thing.

John Brine died in 1829, leaving James to help care for his mother, a younger brother and three young sisters. As soon as James could tell a stone from a potato he worked, even if it was only gathering stones from the fields. In late summer, the whole family worked together to gather in the harvest before it was spoiled by rain. For a short time each year, they had twice their normal earnings and could fill their bellies.

This was James's early life of drudgery and hunger following the cycle of the seasons. In those days there were no buses, railways or planes. Horses pulled the ploughs and provided the fastest transport on land, but only the wealthy rode them. James Brine probably never went far from Tolpuddle.

Years later, Laurie Lee described the country way of life. 'Myself, my family, my generation, were born in a world of silence; a world of hard work and necessary patience, of backs bent to the ground, hands massaging the crops, of waiting on weather and growth; of villages like ships in the empty landscapes and the long walking distances between them...'

Today, we are used to being able to get from one place to another very quickly. We are used to being able to speak to people the other side of the world by telephone; to seeing the news instantly on television. It is hard for us to realize how cut off from the world a village like Tolpuddle was, in James's time. In those days you learned the news from newspapers, days after it happened. If you couldn't read or couldn't afford the newspaper, you listened to rumours told by one person to another, rumours that grew more fantastic with every telling.

When James Brine was a young man, the talk in Dorset was of new-fangled machines used by farmers to drive down wages, and the reply given them by the mysterious and terrible 'Captain Swing'.

Chapter 2

Captain Swing

ONE machine can do the work of many men or women. That is the point of them. Nowadays, many machines are completely automatic or computer controlled, and do not need workers to tend them at all. The early machines needed people to work them, but not nearly so many people as would be needed to do the same job by hand.

Richard Trevithick, who pioneered the use of steam engines in the mines, said that '...every part of agriculture might be performed by steam; carrying manure for the land, ploughing, harrowing, sowing, reaping, thrashing and grinding'.

In fact, it was only the thrashing, or threshing, machine that was much used in Dorset in James Brine's day. It separated wheat grain from the seed cases or chaff. These machines were large and expensive, but could be hired or shared amongst a number of farmers. The power driving them was more likely to be water or horses than steam, which tended to be unreliable on the farm.

The importance of machines was exaggerated by the rumours that passed for news in the countryside. But just the threat to use machines could be used to keep down wages. 'If you won't work for a shilling,' a farmer might say, 'I'll get a machine and do without you.'

In 1830, there was a very cold winter when many labourers were out of work. They began making threats of their own against the landowners and their machines. Nobody wanted to be known by name as a troublemaker, for fear of what might be done to them. Letters of protest were delivered in the dead of night, and signed 'Captain Swing'. Here is a typically menacing but confused Swing letter.

'We understand you be about to put up your Thrashing Maschaine as you cannot afford to pay men to thrash as you ought. Although you be such a man of consequence, if you dare put up that cursed Mashine you may depend on it fire shall be the consequence and I hope to god that you will feel the Heat. Show this to your Pot [drinking] companions who has Thrashing Machines. It saves us the trouble transmitting to them as it makes no difference to us where they go by water or steam. I hope you will take warning by this and not give us the trouble to call on you. Employ the poor to Thrash with the Flail as they used to do; do not waste to much of your bravery or you will come down with your Machine.

(signed) Swing'

The mysterious Captain was said to ride through the countryside causing riots. He almost certainly never existed as a real person. Letters in his name appeared right across the country, and he could not have been everywhere at once!

In his name, threshing machines were broken, hayricks were set alight. Country houses were burgled and some of the gentry were attacked by mobs. Here is a description issued by Cambridge magistrates of a wanted man seen 'SETTING FIRE to a STACK OF OATS'.

'...a tall Man, about 5 feet 10 in. [177 cm] high, sandy whiskers, large red nose, apparently between 50 and 60 years of age. Wore at the time a snuff-colored straight coat, light colored pantaloons, and low shoes.'

They could arrest half the county on this description, but not the dashing and romantic Captain Swing!

Unrest in the countryside reached Tolpuddle, and brings into our tale the magistrate, James Frampton.

Frampton lived at Moreton Hall, and his job as a magistrate was to try people accused of crimes. He himself was a landowner and a wealthy man. This is how his sister Mary described Christmas dinner in her diary, at a time when working people around them were starving.

'...the yule log blazed on the large hearth... the peacock in full plumage was placed on the dinner table with the boar's head... the immense candles were well covered with laurel... and the Wassail bowl and lamb's wool [both festive drinks] were not inferior to former years.'

James Frampton seems to have gone out of his way to confront the protestors, as he later went out of his way to trap James Brine. He gathered a force of farmers and special constables to go with him to a meeting with the labourers. The usual request for fair wages was made by the labourers, quite peacefully, according to Mary.

'The mob, urged on from behind hedges and trees by a number of women and children, advanced rather respectfully, and with their hats in their hands, to demand increase of wages, but would not listen to the request that they would disperse. The Riot Act was read. They still urged forwards, and came up close to Mr Frampton's horse; he then collared one man, but in giving him in charge

he [the man] slipped from his captors by
leaving his smock-frock in their hands.'

Mary wanted to show her brother in the best
light, even in her diary, but we can see the truth
behind her words. The timid labourers were
urged on by their hungry families. Looking down
with contempt from the imposing height of his
horse, James Frampton refused to discuss wages
at all.

The Riot Act that Mary mentions is a law that
made it unlawful for people to gather together to
cause a disturbance. Reading the Riot Act
warned the labourers that violence would be used
against them if they did not go away.

When the crowd, which Mary calls a mob,
would not go away Frampton ordered the police
to charge. They attacked what Mary admitted
was a group of rather respectful men with their
hats in their hands! Three men were arrested for
rioting, but the riot was started by James
Frampton, not by the labourers.

James Frampton became very unpopular. He
blocked up the windows of Moreton Hall, and

sent for the army to protect him and his property. The farmers and landowners were deeply afraid that labourers no longer knew their place. They were afraid of a revolution like the one in France, where the common people had executed their nobility with the infamous guillotine.

So, magistrates such as James Frampton dealt harshly with labourers tried in their courts for 'Swing' offences. In Dorset, thirteen were transported for life. Across the whole of southern England 500 were transported, and nineteen were executed by hanging. Ringleaders were singled out for punishment in order to set an example. There were so many people involved that it would have been difficult to act against them all.

Today, no government could make itself so unpopular. In those days, most people in the countryside were not even allowed to vote. Only property owners could vote for a Member of Parliament, or be elected to parliament themselves. Labourers had no power over the making or enforcing of laws.

James Brine was eighteen at the time of Captain Swing. He took no part in the disturbances, although he must have been as hungry as anyone. James and his friends were known to be good and honest workers.

The awful convict ship that will carry James Brine away from home and family is drawing closer. His life of slavery in Australia is looming on the horizon. It will happen soon, but first we meet his childhood sweetheart, Elizabeth Standfield.

Elizabeth

Standfield

JAMES Brine and Elizabeth Standfield knew
each other from childhood. This was bound
to happen in a village as small as Tolpuddle,
even though Elizabeth was several years younger
than James.

Elizabeth must have had the dark Celtic good
looks of Dorset girls. It was not long before she
caught James's eye. When childhood friendship
grew into teenage romance, he wanted an excuse
to see her at home.

Elizabeth's father Thomas was a Methodist
preacher, as well as a farm labourer. Methodism
is a form of Christianity that broke away from

the main Church of England. James Brine did not have the same religious beliefs as the Standfields, so he could not use that excuse.

But the Standfields were close friends of the Lovelesses. The Loveless brothers, George and James, were also Methodist preachers. Elizabeth Standfield's father was married to their sister Diana. So George and James were Elizabeth's uncles. The Loveless and Standfield families had lived in Tolpuddle for a hundred years. Close family relationships like this were common in such isolated villages.

A friend of the Loveless family was a friend of the Standfields. Luckily for James Brine's romance with Elizabeth, there were several good ways to become a friend of the Lovelesses.

George Loveless was an uneducated ploughman, but he had taught himself to read and write. He ignored his own hunger and spent much of the little he earned on books.

James Brine never went to school, but he was also one of the few labourers who could read and write. George Loveless may have taught him. It was the unselfish sort of thing George would do.

James could then borrow his books, and read and talk about them with Thomas Standfield and his pretty daughter Elizabeth.

Imagine the scene. The cottage is gloomy dark. It is the end of a long, hard day of working in the fields. James's back aches from stooping and digging. He has eaten all he will get today, but he is still hungry.

Shadows from smoky candles flicker on the whitewashed walls. Candles are expensive, so there are not many of them. At the table, James is peering at one of George Loveless's books. He is almost painfully aware of Elizabeth at his shoulder. He turns the pages clumsily with his callused fingers and they read aloud the latest ideas about how all people are equal in the sight of God.

The words make James nervous. The vicar preaches in church that everyone has their place in the world, from the highest to the lowest. He says that it is wrong to try to change things.

George Loveless wants to change things. He preaches to whoever will listen, out in the open air. He says that even the lowest in the land have a right to a living wage for themselves and their families.

When James's stomach growls with hunger, he wonders if George is right. He turns and looks into Elizabeth's dark eyes and wonders what it will be like to be married, and to have children of his own. There may be five or six, or even more of them. How will he feed them on a labourer's pay? How will he buy their clothes? Where will they live?

As he realises how hopeless the task of caring for a family will be, James knows that George Loveless is right.

'It's not fair!' James thinks. 'All my life I'll work hard and earn little. My children will starve while the children of farmers and landowners grow fat. Are they really better than us? Do they deserve more? No, rich people hardly work at all! Landowners inherit their money and land. They're only lucky to be born into rich families. They could pay their labourers more and still have plenty themselves.'

James Brine is nervous because, in the 1800s, these ideas are dangerous. They come close to what is called sedition – trying to overthrow the government. People are hanged for sedition.

As James reads with Elizabeth and her father, bands of desperate men are roaming in the Dorset night, breaking machines and burning hayricks in the name of Captain Swing. They only want a living wage for themselves and their families, but they too can be hanged for riot, robbery and violence.

But George Loveless never encourages anyone to break the law. The Lovelesses and the Standfields are God-fearing, law-abiding people who have nothing to do with such things. James respects them, and wants to be like them. He wants the dark-eyed Elizabeth. Will his dreams come true?

George Loveless

IN every gathering of people there are those who stand out from the crowd, and not just because of their physical appearance. Perhaps they speak well, or know a lot, or come from respected families. Other people turn to them for leadership.

George Loveless was such a born leader. He was short at 162 cm, but his work as a ploughman must have made him strong. He had the dark hair and swarthy skin of many Dorset folk. He and his brother James were used to speaking in public, and when the villagers of Tolpuddle needed someone to speak up for them, they found George Loveless.

The 'Swing' riots had been ruthlessly put down by magistrates such as James Frampton, with no improvement in life for ordinary country folk. Then in 1832, a peaceful dispute over pay began in Tolpuddle. Before it was over, James Brine would be carried away from Dorset and around the world.

A meeting was called between the labourers, the farmers and landowners to talk about pay. This first meeting was peaceful. As George Loveless later wrote, '...they came to a mutual agreement, the masters in Tolpuddle promising to give the men as much for their labour as other masters in the district. The whole of the men then went to their work, and the time that was spent in this affair did not exceed two hours. No language of intimidation or threatening was used on the occasion.'

The employers paid nine shillings a week for a while. The labourers accepted this, even though it meant abject poverty. It cost half as much again for a family to pay its rent, eat and buy fuel, as this budget of the time shows.

WAGES OF DESPAIR
Average family expenditure (1840s)

ITEM	PRICE
Rent	1s 2d
Bread	9s
Tea	2d
Potatoes	1s
Sugar	3s 5d
Soap	3d
Thread	2.5d
Candles	3d
Salt	0.5d
Coal and Wood	9d
Butter	4.5d
Cheese	3d
TOTAL	13s 9d

Wages of 9 or 10 shillings a week reduced families to starvation level unless they could be supplemented by working wives and children.

The Rector of Barkham described the lives of rural labourers and their families:

> 'Many working men breakfast and dine on dry bread alone, without cheese or drink of any kind; their meal is supper, and generally no better than unpeeled potatoes and salt, or barley-cake fried, and water. Clothes they get as they can, and the children go nearly naked. There is little work now for lads, and that at a reduced price; 2d or 3d a day...'

So when the Tolpuddle employers went back on their word and put wages down to eight shillings a week, the labourers called for another meeting to ask them to stick to their agreement.

A local magistrate was asked to run the meeting and make it official. This magistrate was none other than James Frampton, landowner and scourge of the Swing rioters! He had no sympathy for the plight of the poor.

George Loveless acted as spokesman for the

labourers, but it was no good. Later, he wrote:
'...we were told that we must work for what our
employers thought fit to give us, as there was no
law to compel masters to give any fixed sum of
money to their servants.'

The farmers and landowners denied that there
had been an agreement reached at the earlier
meeting. The labourers called upon the vicar as
witness, but he denied it too. Very soon wages
were reduced to seven shillings a week, and then
even further to six shillings!

This must have been a punishment for asking
for more, like little Oliver in Charles Dickens's
book *Oliver Twist*. How could people be so
cruel? What could the labourers do, as George
Loveless says, 'knowing it was impossible to live
honestly on such scanty means'?

They might have chosen to live dishonestly, by
poaching, burglary or robbery. But this was not
the way of the Lovelesses and the Standfields, or
their young friend James Brine.

Meetings were held under the great sycamore
tree that still grows in the village. George
Loveless had heard about unions, and he found

out more from a brother living in London. It was decided to organize a trade union for the farm labourers of Tolpuddle.

Members of a trade union agree to follow its rules, and the most important rule is that they act together. Then the union can get better wages for everybody, than the workers could if they acted alone.

The members of a union help each other. Those in work pay money each week, to give to those who have no work.

In the early days there were also strict rules of secrecy. This was because employers hated the unions and tried to break them up, although they had no right to do this. Unions were made legal in 1824, and by the 1830s there were several in the industrial towns of England, though none for workers in the countryside. One of the biggest unions sent members to the next meeting in Tolpuddle, to give advice.

James Brine was there. Imagine his excitement! Forty labourers crammed into Thomas Standfield's little cottage. The air was thick with smoke. George and Thomas were at the front, welcoming the visitors from faraway London. The talk was full of grand-sounding words like 'justice', 'solidarity' and a 'fair wage'.

The Tolpuddle Friendly Society of Agricultural Labourers was created. The rules were copied from existing unions in the north. One rule in particular shows that the labourers' aims were peaceful: '…any act of violence' or other breaking of the law was forbidden, as it would '…injure the cause and destroy the society itself'.

Guardians were appointed whose job was to keep meetings safe from spies. Members would be let in only if they knew the secret password, which was 'Either Hand or Heart'. They had to swear an oath of secrecy as part of a solemn initiation ceremony, designed to impress them and make them loyal to each other and to the union.

It was just this ceremony that was the downfall of the Tolpuddle union and its leading members, including young James Brine. For, despite all their vigilance, there were spies in their midst.

Chapter 5

Spies!

YOU are led up a creaking wooden stairway. At the top you are blindfolded and led into an upstairs room. You stumble and are supported by unseen hands. All around is the soft sound of breathing and the small movements of many people.

'Kneel.'

A familiar voice speaks with awesome authority.

'O God, who art the author of peace and lover of concord, defend us in this our undertaking, that we may not fear the power of our adversaries...'

The words seem to be from the Bible, but they are hard to understand. A dig in the ribs prompts you to join in the 'Amen' at the end.

Strong hands hoist you to your feet and pull the blindfold away. The scene that meets your eyes makes you catch your breath and sway with dizziness.

A looming skeleton is raising a scythe to cut off your head! You cry out in fear!

'Remember thine end,' says a solemn voice.

By the flickering light of candles you see that the skeleton is a huge painting on the wall. You are surrounded by people you knew, but no longer know.

They are wearing gowns like the vicar wears in church. Their faces are stern and unsmiling. They are like strangers, but they treat you as the stranger, chanting:

'Stranger, *within our secret walls we have admitted you,*
Hoping you will prove honest, faithful, just and true,
If you cannot keep the secrets we require,

Go hence, you are at liberty to retire.
Are your motives pure?'

You swallow hard, and answer, 'Yes.'

The ceremony continues for so long that you lose track of time. Much of what is said you do not understand. Your eyes wander around the room. On a table there are papers and a large book.

Suddenly, you are blindfolded again. Hands pull you round and round the room until you hardly know where you are. Booted feet stamp the bare boards. The noise is deafening!

The din stops and your hand is placed on the book.

'Kiss the Bible.'

The blindfold is taken away and you repeat a long oath, a few words at a time.

'...I will persevere in endeavouring to support
a brotherhood known by the name of the
Friendly Society of Agricultural Labourers,
and I solemnly declare and promise that I
will never act in opposition to the

brotherhood in any of their attempts to support wages, but will, to the utmost of my power, assist them in all lawful and just occasions, to obtain a fair remuneration [pay] for our labour... if ever I reveal either part or parts of this my most solemn obligation, may all the Society I am about to belong to, and all that is just, disgrace me so long as I live; and may what is now before me plunge my soul into the everlasting pit of misery. Amen.'

James Brine went through this initiation ceremony and swore the oath of loyalty to the Tolpuddle labourers and their union. Many secret societies use ceremonies like this. It was dramatic stuff, a bit of theatre to make James keep secret the names of the members and officers of the union, and what they intended to do about wages.

If the farmers and landowners knew these things, they would almost certainly refuse to give work to the union's leaders and would turn them out of their homes. As it was, they gave as much work as they could to labourers who were not in the union.

About half the labourers in Tolpuddle were members of the Friendly Society of Agricultural Labourers. They asked for the same pay that labourers got outside Tolpuddle - nine or ten shillings a week. This was what the farmers agreed to pay at the very first meeting between labourers and employers. Labourers who were not in the union worked for whatever they were offered.

The farmers and landowners in Tolpuddle became more and more worried. Some wanted to give in, but there was one who would never give in. This was the magistrate, James Frampton.

Frampton knew about the union meetings, and he wanted them stopped and the leaders arrested. But unions were perfectly legal, and he was struggling to find a way to do these things.

Why was he so set against the Tolpuddle labourers?

It seems that they went against what he thought was the right and proper way for servants to act towards their masters. James

Frampton loved king and country. Perhaps he feared that the common people might press for a republic like that in France, if unions were not ruthlessly stamped upon.

The Tolpuddle unionists did not want to get rid of the king. They only wanted better wages so that their families would have enough to eat.

The story of James Brine and his friends has become a legend that is told over and over again. They are called the Tolpuddle Martyrs, because of the sacrifices they made.

The Martyrs themselves were humble people who only wanted to improve the lives of labourers in Tolpuddle. Why were they so important to the rest of the country, and to history itself?

The fate of the Tolpuddle Friendly Society of Agricultural Labourers was vital to the future of working people everywhere. If Magistrate Frampton found a way to crush this new union in the countryside, the way would be open to crush the older unions in the towns.

Every so often, there are times in history when events can move in a number of different ways.

This was one of those important times. In one direction lay continuing poverty for most people, in what we now call wage-slavery. In another direction lay power for ordinary people, and what we understand as democracy.

All this depended on the contest between James Frampton and the six Tolpuddle Martyrs. He had the might of the law on his side. They had only courage and their faith in true justice.

Frampton asked for help from the government minister in charge of law and order: the Home Secretary, Lord Melbourne. Frampton wrote to his Lordship about these 'combinations [the Tolpuddle union] of a dangerous and alarming kind'. He had no proof as yet of lawbreaking, but he hoped that his spies – 'Trusty persons' – would get the evidence he needed.

This is what James Frampton's letter said. 'As no specific proof of the time or place of these meetings or of the individuals forming them, have as yet reached the Justices so as to authorise them to take measures to interrupt the meetings or to notice [arrest] the persons engaged in them; all they have been able to do at present has been to communicate with Trusty persons in the neighbourhood and by their means endeavour to trace the proceedings and identify the parties.'

Who were these spies? Their names were Edward Legg and John Lock. Young James Brine made the mistake of recruiting them for the union!

James only wanted to help. He knew that the more labourers there were in the union, the more powerful it would be. If employers could not find anyone else to do their work, they would have to pay higher wages to the union members.

So when James met John Lock, he asked him to come to a meeting. He should have known better. Lock worked as a gardener for James Frampton!

John Lock refused to go that time. When James asked him again a couple of weeks later, he agreed. Had Lock talked to his employer in the meantime, and had Frampton told him to spy on the union for him?

But James Brine was pleased. He and his friend James Hammett led a little band of recruits to John Standfield's house. The recruits were John Lock and four others, including Edward Legg.

They were initiated together on 9 December 1833, with the ceremony of blindfolds, Bible and oath. Then Lock and Legg told everything they could remember to James Frampton.

The spies were frightened men. Their stories were never very clear, except on one thing – that they had taken a secret oath. That was the excuse the magistrate found to send James Brine and his friends as convicts to Australia for seven years.

C h a p t e r   6

Gaol!

T HE village constable arrested the leaders of
the Tolpuddle union early in the morning
of 24 February 1834. The six were George
Loveless and his younger brother James,
Thomas Standfield and his son John, James
Hammett and, of course, young James Brine.

'Are you willing to go to the magistrates with
me?' asked the constable.

'To any place wherever you wish me,'
answered George Loveless.

They all walked the seven miles to
Dorchester. If the Tolpuddle men had refused
the constable could not have forced them, for

he was alone and unarmed. But why should they refuse?

'We've done no wrong,' James Brine must have been thinking. 'Somebody has made a mistake. We'll be home as soon as it is sorted out.'

Little did he know that George Loveless had evidence of a serious crime in his pocket. Neither did George.

They were taken to the house of the magistrate Charles Woolaston. Also present was Woolaston's half-brother – none other than James Frampton! – and Edward Legg. The spy swore that he had been initiated into the union with a secret oath in Thomas Standfield's cottage by these Tolpuddle men. The six were sent to Dorchester Gaol.

There they were stripped and searched. Their heads were shaved and they were made to wear prison clothes, as if they had already been tried and found guilty!

James Brine was confused and frightened. George Loveless had told him that the union was lawful. How could these awful things be happening?

They were happening because Magistrate Frampton had found a way to trap the leaders of the Tolpuddle union.

Unions as such were not illegal, but secret oaths were. So a union that used secret oaths was illegal. This was Frampton's twisted thinking, using advice given him by the Home Secretary.

Secret oaths were sworn by many societies at the time. The law making secret oaths illegal was an old one that hardly anyone knew about. It was intended to stop mutinies in the navy. It was never intended to be used against unions.

The magistrates were stretching the law as far as it could go, to catch honest people who did not know they had done wrong. Unfortunately, a copy of a notice was found in George Loveless's pocket that seemed to prove he did know that secret oaths were illegal.

Just three days before the arrests, James Frampton had ordered a notice or CAUTION to be put up in Tolpuddle. This notice used lots of long and difficult words.

'...that mischievous and designing Persons have been for some time past, endeavouring to induce [persuade], and have induced many Labourers in various Parishes in this County, to attend Meetings, and to enter into Illegal Societies or Unions, to which they bind themselves by **unlawful oaths, administered** [given] **secretly** by Persons concealed, who artfully deceive the ignorant and unwary...'
Anyone who swore a secret oath, or persuaded someone else to swear one, the notice said, '...Will become Guilty of Felony, and be liable to be Transported for Seven Years'.

George Loveless freely admitted, 'I met with a copy, read it, and put it into my pocket.'

The CAUTION used the tricky language of lawyers. We have added the emphasis on **unlawful oaths, administered secretly**. It was not there to help George Loveless. Would a labourer who had taught himself to read realise how important this was? Even if he did, it was an awful injustice! James and his friends were arrested for breaking laws that only lawyers knew about.

George Loveless could have emptied his pockets on the seven mile walk from Tolpuddle to Dorchester. They were guarded by just one constable. How easy it would have been to crumple up the notice. How simple to throw the ball of paper into a hedgerow when the constable was not looking.

But George was a man of principle. He believed in his own innocence and in the innocence of his companions. He kept the notice in his pocket all the long way to Dorchester. There, his gaolers seized it, along with the key to the union strong box.

In the strong box was a list of the union's members, but Frampton was only interested in the leaders – James Brine and his friends.

The gaol was horrible. George Loveless said: '...As soon as we arrived we were ushered down some steps into a miserable dungeon, opened but twice a year, with only a glimmering light...' Each man was locked into his own tiny windowless cell, '...and to make it more disagreeable, some wet and green brushwood was served for firing. The smoke of this place, together with its natural dampness, amounted to nearly suffocation...'

James Brine and his friends were tried at the County Hall in Dorchester. They were deeply afraid for themselves and for their families. If they were found guilty, who would look after their wives and children? James was worried about Elizabeth, as well as his own family. If Elizabeth's father Thomas was sent to prison, she and her family could be thrown out of their home. Without both Thomas and John Standfield's earnings, Elizabeth's pregnant mother and four younger children might end up in the workhouse!

At the trial, both John Lock and Edward Legg said that James Brine and James Hammett took them to John Standfield's cottage, where they swore the secret oath. James Brine was sorry he had trusted the magistrate's gardener!

George Loveless's words to the court were, 'My Lord, if we have violated any law, it was not done intentionally: we have injured no man's reputation, character, person, or property: we were uniting together to preserve ourselves, our wives, and our children, from utter degradation and starvation.'

This plea was not enough to save them. The jury took only twenty minutes to decide that the labourers were guilty. Judge Baron Williams gave them the heaviest sentence he could, saying, 'The use of all punishment is not with a view to the particular offenders or for the sake of revenge... it is for the sake of example...'

The Judge and the magistrates wanted to make it impossible in future for any union to get members. This was the 'example' that Baron Williams spoke about. Who would join a union and risk seven years' transportation?

Today, even those who do not like unions agree that workers often need help in getting a fair wage. Magistrate James Frampton and Judge Baron Williams condemned labourers and their families to poverty, starvation, and early death.

George and James Loveless, Thomas and John Standfield, James Hammett – and James Brine – fought to save themselves and their fellows from this awful fate. In doing so, they suffered an awful fate themselves. They would be humiliated, starved and tortured. They would be separated from their loved ones for years. This is how they earned the name of the Tolpuddle Martyrs.

Chapter 7

Convict ships

God is our guide, from field, from wave,
From plough, from anvil, and from loom;
We come, our country's rights to save,
And speak a tyrant faction's doom:
We raise the watch-word liberty:
We will, we will, we will be free.

God is our guide! No swords we draw,
We kindle not war's battle fires:
By reason, union, justice, law,
We claim the birth-right of our sires:
We raise the watch-word liberty:
We will, we will, we will be free!

These were the defiant words written by George Loveless (though not composed by him) on a piece of paper that he threw into the crowd outside Dorchester County Hall. They became famous as the 'Song of Freedom'. (The music for this song is on page 121.)

The Martyrs were marched back to Dorchester gaol, where George Loveless was struck down by a fever. He blamed this on the terrible conditions in the dungeon. Whilst George was in the prison hospital, James and the others had irons fixed to their legs and wrists. They were seated on the outside of a horse-drawn coach, and chained together as well as to the coach.

Tossed to and fro by every pothole in the road, freezing cold in the raw March air, they were driven to the naval town of Portsmouth. There they were taken on board the hulks, leaky and rotten prison ships without masts or sails that would never again leave port.

James Brine, James Hammett and both Standfields were taken on board the *York*, and James Loveless on to the *Leviathan*. They had to put on convict clothes of coarse grey cloth, with flat hats and stiff, badly fitting boots. Their chains were replaced by heavier and even more uncomfortable ones.

Life aboard the hulks was like hell, as an earlier prisoner named James Hardy Vaux had told. 'There were confined in this floating dungeon nearly six hundred men, most of them double-ironed; and the reader may conceive of the horrible effects arising from the continual rattle of chains, the filth and vermin naturally produced by such a crew of miserable inhabitants, the oaths and execrations [curses] constantly heard among them... Nothing short of a descent into the infernal regions can be at all worthy of comparison with it...'

Young James was frightened of the guards, who Vaux said were 'brutal by nature, and rendered more tyrannical and cruel by consciousness of [knowing] the power they possess'. They beat the prisoners with sticks and flogged them with whips at the smallest excuse. Salt was rubbed into bleeding backs, and the pain of this was worse than the flogging itself.

James was almost as frightened of the other prisoners, who had become hardened by the battle to survive. On the hulks, Vaux said, 'a man will rob his best benefactor or even messmate, of an article worth one halfpenny'. All were hungry and many were sick. Few lived long.

James was lucky. He had true friends who shared his ordeal, and in two days they were all (including James Loveless) moved to the *Surrey*. This was not a rotting hulk, but a sea-worthy vessel that would take them to Australia.

They had a slow start. For nine days the *Surrey* was anchored at Plymouth to take on food and more convicts. Then they sailed out into open seas.

Few of the convicts had been to sea before, and most were seasick. Even so, they were allowed on deck only for two hours in the morning and two in the afternoon. The rest of the time they were chained up, six men to a tiny cell only two metres in each direction. There was not enough room to lie down!

James sat, huddled in his thin blanket, feeling utterly miserable. The food, when he could eat it, was horrible. It was like the 'smiggins' he had been given on the prison hulk – salt beef boiled with barley to make a mess like glue. There was little enough of it. Convicts ate 'six upon four', which is to say, six convicts shared as much food as was given to four sailors.

Harsh measures were used to keep this desperate human cargo from mutiny. The iron chains were heavy and could be weighted down even more as punishment. There was a spy hole in the cell door through which the guard could fire his musket at the first sign of trouble.

Troublemakers would be branded with a red-hot iron, and flogged with the cat-o'-nine tails. This whip was made of leather and wire, and tipped with lead. After flogging, the half-dead prisoner was forced into the 'coffin bath', full of salt water.

No wonder the convicts were desperate! John Standfield wrote, 'I then began to feel the misery of transportation – confined down with a number of the most degraded and wretched criminals, each man having to contend [fight] with his fellow or be trodden underfoot.'

The Tolpuddle Martyrs avoided trouble. Not all the convicts were hardened criminals. Some had stolen something small, some were guilty of nothing at all, and women and children were amongst their number.

George Loveless recovered from his illness and left England shortly after the others, on the convict ship *William Metcalfe*. Both ships took about four months to reach Australia. They landed at different penal [punishment] settlements.

George was taken to the island called Van Diemen's Land (now Tasmania) off mainland Australia. A popular song of the same name helped spread its fearful reputation.

*Come all you gallant poachers that ramble free
    from care,
That walk out on moonlight nights, with your
    dog, gun and snare,
The jolly hares and pheasants, you have at
    your command,
Not thinking that your last career is to Van
    Diemen's Land.*

*The first day that we landed upon this fatal
    shore*
*The planters they came round us, full twenty
    score or more,*
*They rank'd us up like horses, and sold us out
    of hand,*
*And yok'd us up to ploughs, my boys, to
    plough Van Diemen's Land.*

*It's often when in slumber I have a pleasant
    dream,*
*With my sweet girl a-sitting all by a purling
    stream,*
*Through England I've been roaming with her
    at command,*
*Now I awake, broken hearted, upon Van
    Diemen's Land.*

Australia had been used as a huge open prison
for almost fifty years, since 1788. It was intended
that the first penal settlement would be at Botany
Bay. Another popular song taking its name from
the place it described said it was there that 'night
walkers' [poachers] ended their days.

Come all you men of learning,
And a warning take by me,
I would have you quit night-walking,
And shun bad company.
I would have you quit night-walking,
Or else you'll rue the day,
You'll rue your transportation, lads,
When you're bound for Botany Bay.

In fact, Botany Bay was not fit even for a penal settlement, and the convict ships sailed further north to the beautiful natural harbour of Sydney in New South Wales. This is where James Brine and his fellows aboard the *Surrey* were taken.

Chapter 8

Australia— New South Wales

JAMES Brine staggered on to the quay at Sydney. For weeks aboard the Surrey he had been seasick. but in the end he found his 'sea-legs'. Now he could not walk on solid land: the ground seemed to be heaving beneath his feet like the deck of the ship!

All convicts were first examined by a doctor, and a government official. They wrote down a description of each prisoner, paying close attention to scars and suchlike. In the days before photography, the description would help the warders know who was who, if anyone tried to run away. James was described like this:

'Brine Jas; Aged 21; Education – R.W. [can read and write]; Religion – Protestant; Unmarried; Native place – Dorsetshire; Trade – farm servant; Offence – unlawful oaths; Tried – Dorset Assizes, 14 March, 1833; Sentence – 7 years; Previous convictions – none; Height – 5 ft 5 ins [165 cm]; Complexion – ruddy; Hair – brown; Eyes – hazel/grey; Physical details – scar right eyebrow. Scar under left nostril. Scar back of left thumb. Scars on face and one back of middle finger of left hand.'

Poor James already had more scars than most of us get in a lifetime! He got most of them as a farm labourer in Tolpuddle. He was used to rough hard work. Just as well, for there was plenty of that in Australia!

New South Wales was now a colony. Free settlers had come from England to be farmers and Sydney had grown into a small town. Compared to Tolpuddle, of course, Sydney was big, but it was just a town in a clearing in the forest, which is called 'the bush'. The farms that colonists had carved out of the bush were far apart and connected by little more than tracks.

Australia was a strange place seen through the eyes of an inexperienced English farm labourer. It was raw, wild and dangerous – very different to Dorset! When James left the convict ship in September it was sunny and hot, and would get hotter. This was springtime, south of the Equator.

The aborigines who are native to Australia were hunter-gatherers, as some still are today. They live off the bush. They do not keep animals or grow crops like British farmers. They kill wild game and pick wild fruits.

Many trees in the bush are hundreds of metres high, draped with vines, and with parasitic plants growing in their canopies. When they fall, lurid fungi consume them, and canes and ferns fill the space.

And the birds! Flocks of gaudy parrots add their squawks to the clicks and whistles of unseen forest animals. There is even a bird – the lyrebird – that imitates everyone else. That sound of chopping, that cough and sneeze, is not a person. It's the lyrebird!

A convict was the property of the British government. The governors in Australia usually sold them to the colonists like slaves. The farmers could do what they wanted with the convict labourers. They could treat them well, or badly. They could starve them and beat them for real and imaginary wrongdoing. Running away was punished by brutal flogging whilst tied to an iron triangle.

A convict who continued to offend was put to backbreaking work mending roads on a chain gang, or sent to one of the penal settlements for special punishment. These were described by a convict named Joseph Holt as 'the dwelling of devils in human shape, the refuse of Botany Bay, the doubly damned'. Convicts everywhere were hungry all the time. This drove them to steal and to eat anything they could. A cat made a good meal!

James Brine was sold to Robert Scott, who had a farm inland at Hunter's River, near Glindon.

CAUTION.

WHEREAS it has been represented to us from several quarters, that mischievous and designing Persons have been for some time past, endeavouring to induce, and have induced, many Labourers in various Parishes in this County, to attend Meetings, and to enter into Illegal Societies or Unions, to which they bind themselves by unlawful oaths, administered secretly by Persons concealed, who artfully deceive the ignorant and unwary,—WE, the undersigned Justices think it our duty to give this PUBLIC NOTICE and CAUTION, that all Persons may know the danger they incur by entering into such Societies.

ANY PERSON who shall become a Member of such a Society, or take any Oath, or assent to any Test or Declaration not authorized by Law—

Any Person who shall administer, or be present at, or consenting to the administering or taking any Unlawful Oath, or who shall cause such Oath to be administered, although not actually present at the time—

Any Person who shall not reveal or discover any Illegal Oath which may have been administered, or any Illegal Act done or to be done—

Any Person who shall induce, or endeavour to persuade any other Person to become a Member of such Societies,

WILL BECOME

Guilty of Felony,

AND BE LIABLE TO BE

Transported for Seven Years.

ANY PERSON who shall be compelled to take such an Oath, unless he shall declare the same within four days, together with the whole of what he shall know touching the same, will be liable to the same Penalty.

Any Person who shall directly or indirectly maintain correspondence or intercourse with such Society, will be deemed Guilty of an Unlawful Combination and Confederacy, and on Conviction before one Justice, on the Oath of one Witness, be liable to a Penalty of TWENTY POUNDS, or to be committed to the Common Gaol or House of Correction, for THREE CALENDAR MONTHS ; or if proceeded against by Indictment, may be CONVICTED OF FELONY, and be TRANSPORTED FOR SEVEN YEARS.

Any Person who shall knowingly permit any Meeting of any such Society to be held in any House, Building, or other Place, shall for the first offence be liable to the Penalty of FIVE POUNDS ; and for every other offence committed after Conviction, be deemed Guilty of such Unlawful Combination and Confederacy, and on Conviction before one Justice, on the Oath of one Witness, be liable to a Penalty of TWENTY POUNDS, or to Commitment to the Common Gaol or House of Correction, FOR THREE CALENDAR MONTHS ; or if proceeded against by Indictment may be

CONVICTED OF FELONY,
And Transported for SEVEN YEARS.

| COUNTY OF DORSET, *Dorchester Division.* February 22d. 1834. | C. B. WOLLASTON, JAMES FRAMPTON, WILLIAM ENGLAND, THOS. DADE, JNO. MORTON COLSON, | HENRY FRAMPTON, RICHD. TUCKER STEWARD, WILLIAM R. CHURCHILL, AUGUSTUS FOSTER. |

G. CLARK, PRINTER, CORNHILL, DORCHESTER.

Picture 1: The Caution against 'Illegal Societies or Unions' and 'unlawful oaths' that was displayed in Tolpuddle. You can see the names of James Frampton, his son Henry Frampton, and his half-brother C.B. Wollaston, at the bottom. The Caution is discussed on page 48.

The Political Drama. No. 32.

THE DORCHESTER UNIONISTS IMPLORING MERCY !!! OF THEIR KING,

"He who trusts in Parvotea shall be thus rewarded":-

Printed and Published by G. Drake, 12, Houghton Street, Clare Market.

Picture 2: A cartoon published at the time of the Tolpuddle Martyrs' trial. It shows the six men pleading for mercy from King William IV, who has turned his back on them. The woman is the King's wife, Queen Adelaide. The man on the right is almost certainly the King's brother, the Duke of Cumberland, who is ordering the guards to take the men away and transport them.

Picture 3: A contemporary engraving of the Copenhagen Fields demonstration in London, on Monday 21 April 1834. It was part of a nation-wide campaign to pardon the Tolpuddle men, and is described on page 88.

Picture 4: A festival is held in Tolpuddle, Dorset every July, with speakers, music and exhibitions. Trade unionists and their families march through the village with their banners, in memory of the Tolpuddle Martyrs.

James had to find his own way there from Sydney. Why didn't he run away, and simply disappear into this strange new land?

Convicts did not know how to find wild food, the way the aborigines did. Most runaways in Australia starved until they gave themselves up, and were then brutally flogged. Some joined the bushrangers – armed outlaws who roamed the forest, preying on settlers and convicts alike. Government soldiers hunted them down and hanged them if they could.

The most famous bushranger was Ned Kelly, who wore an iron helmet as armour against the guns of the soldiers. Even so he was caught, and in 1880 he was hanged at the age of twenty-five. Many songs were written about him and he became a hero in people's memories, though he was not quite so popular when he was alive!

James Brine was not a criminal and he would not become one. He never forgot that he was innocent. He was determined to survive and see his beloved Elizabeth again.

The journey to Hunter's River started well. This is what James said about it.

'I went on board the steamboat, and reached the green hills the following day. I had then about thirty miles [48 kilometres] to travel on land before reaching the place of my destination. My master had given me at starting a small bed and blanket to take with me, and one shilling to bear my expenses, besides a suit of new slops [work clothes].'

This is the sort of boat ride that modern tourists love. James was glad to be carried along the river. After so many months locked up, just to be out in the open air was like a breath of freedom.

The lack of exercise had made him very unfit. By the time he got off the boat, James was too tired to walk. The bush was dark and menacing. He unrolled his bed and lay down to sleep under a gum-tree. That was when the bushrangers attacked!

Chapter 9

Bushwacked!

THE night was filled with the noise of chirping insects and croaking frogs. The cool air was welcome after the heat of the day. With his bedroll on the hard ground and a warm blanket around him, James was comfortable for the first time in a long while, and he slipped quickly into a deep sleep.

There are all sorts of dangerous animals in Australia. There are deadly poisonous spiders and snakes. James did not know that he was being watched by one of the most dangerous predators in the Australian bush.

The crunch of heavy boots did not wake him.

He was used to sleeping through chains rattling and all sorts of scuffling and banging. The first thing he knew was being hauled to his feet by the scruff of his neck and a pistol thrust under his chin.

There is a saying that there is no honour amongst thieves. The bushrangers were not like Robin Hood, taking from the rich to give to the poor. The bushrangers took from anyone they could and kept it for themselves. James Brine was an easy target camped out alone and defenceless in the bush.

Did they laugh when they saw how little he had, or were they angry? James feared they would kill him. They took everything of value, little though it was: '...the bushrangers came upon me and robbed me of all I possessed, excepting the old clothes I had on, which were given me at Portsmouth'.

His bed, his new clothes, his boots and his money were gone, but he was alive. Calling on all his reserves of strength, James walked barefoot forty-eight kilometres along rough tracks in the blazing sun. He staggered into

Mr Scott's farm 'exhausted from want of food, having had but one meal in three days'.

Was the master sympathetic? He was not! James said later:

> 'I was instantly taken by the overseer to the master, who asked me where my slops [work clothes] and bedding were. I told him that the bushrangers had robbed me; but he swore that I was a liar, and said that he would give me a 'D——d good flogging' in the morning.'

Mr Scott thought that James was 'one of the Dorsetshire machine-breakers' (which was not true), and was determined to punish him. He sent James away with no food, hungry though the boy was.

He did seem to forget about the flogging, for the next morning James was set to digging post-holes for fences. After his ordeal, James was not fit for work and apologized to his master: 'I told him I was doing as well as I could, but was unable to do much through weakness, and that, having walked so far without shoes, my feet were so cut and sore I could not put them to the spade.'

He might have shouted down a well, for all the good this did him. Mr Scott replied: 'If you utter another word of complaint, I will put you in the lock-up; and if you ask me for an article for six months to come, or if you do not your work like another man, or do not attend to the overseer's orders, whatever they may be, I will send you up to Mr Moody, where no mercy shall be shown you.'

Mr Moody was the man with the whip!

So James had to struggle on, with bleeding feet, dressed in rags that hardly kept off the sun, no bed to sleep on and weak from hunger. He was given new clothes only when the stolen ones would have worn out, if he had been wearing them.

James had to dig with bare feet, or be sent to the dreadful Mr Moody. He cleverly solved the problem: 'I afterwards got a piece of an iron hoop and wrapped [it] round my foot to tread upon, and for six months, until I became due [for new clothes], I went without shoes, clothes or bedding, and lay on the bare ground at night.'

After working up to his chest in water for more than a fortnight, washing sheep, James caught a bad cold. He begged for a blanket to keep himself warm at night, even 'if it were only a piece of horse-cloth'. He was refused again.

Mr Scott mistook James for one of the Swing rioters, who broke threshing machines and burned hayricks in the early 1830s.

'What would your masters in England have had to cover them if you had not been sent here?' he ranted. 'I understand it was your intention to have murdered, burnt and destroyed every thing before you, and you are sent over here to be severely punished, and no mercy shall be shown you.'

James was completely in this man's power.

'If you ask for any thing before the six months is expired [up], I will flog you as often as I like.'

When James told his master that unions did not murder, burn or destroy anything, Mr Scott asked all about them. He wasn't really interested or being friendly. He just wanted James to inform on his friends.

James refused, of course, and Mr Scott became very angry. 'Don't you know that not even a hair on your head is your own. Go to your hut, or I will well kick you.'

Somehow, James had to survive. His strengths were his youth, his intelligence, his love for Elizabeth, and the good friends that he would never betray.

He could not actually speak to the other Tolpuddle Martyrs. Australia is a huge continent, and they were far away. Grieving relatives in England did not understand the size of Australia. One convict had to write home to say, 'Please tell poor Mrs Hart [that] it is out of my power to enquire for Henry Hart, as Sydney is 2,000 miles [3,200 kilometres] from me.'

Mrs Hart thought that it was just the town down the road!

The authorities deliberately split the Tolpuddle Martyrs up, and tried to get them to inform on each other. Weaker people would have made something up to get better treatment for themselves, but the Martyrs stood firm. James Hammett said that each had been 'sold like a slave for £1', and they were forced to work like slaves in the heat of Australia.

Thomas Standfield was the oldest of the six. His strength was drained by the sea journey, and he suffered badly as a shepherd in the bush. John Standfield described his father's plight in these words.

'The flocks generally consist of from five to six hundred head of sheep, which the shepherd will have to conduct [lead] into the bush, probably several miles from the farm. The bush is an immense forest of trees and brushwood, with here and there a clear spot of ground, upon which the sheep are driven.

'It frequently happens that prisoners... lose themselves and their flocks... and are several days before they find their way back, during which time they experience great danger and misery, from the fear of meeting with the natives, and from hunger, being only allowed one day's rations when they leave the farm.

'On their return the sheep are counted by the overseer, and should one be missing the shepherd is almost certain to get flogged...'

At first, the Standfields were lucky to be quite close to each other, and John could visit his father. He said that Thomas was 'a dreadful spectacle, covered with sores from head to foot, and weak and helpless as a child'.

The shepherd slept in a 'watch-box' next to his sheep. This was just like a coffin, without a lid! It gave no shelter from any storm. After the flock was settled for the night, John Standfield had to walk seven kilometres to the farm and back for his food. No wonder he was sick and exhausted!

James Loveless and James Hammett also worked hard for their masters in New South Wales. George Loveless was singled out for special treatment by being sent to Van Diemen's Land. The authorities knew that he was the overall leader. They wanted him to betray his fellows and the labourers' union.

Chapter 10

Australia –

Van Diemen's Land

THE island of Van Diemen's Land was a colony in Australia that was even wilder than New South Wales. The hills were higher, the forest was thicker and the aborigines were more troublesome to the foreign invaders. Conditions for convicts were even worse than on the mainland.

The ship carrying George Loveless landed at the island's biggest town, Hobart. His description was recorded, too.

'Loveless Geo; Trade – Ploughman; Height – 5 ft 4 in [162 cm]; Age – 37; Complexion – brown; Head – Small; Hair – Brown; Whiskers

– Dark Red; Visage – small; Forehead – low;
Eyes – Dark hazel; Nose – Small; Mouth –
Med. Wide; Chin – Small Dimpled; Remarks –
Small scar on upper lip, Scar on L. arm;
Native Place – Nr. Dorset.'

George Loveless was questioned several times about the union, to see if he would admit to any treason, or blame other people for breaking the law. He still insisted that all the Tolpuddle men were innocent.

'We meant nothing more, Sir, than uniting together to keep up the price of labour, and to support each other in time of need... for every man that is a member of the Union is under an obligation not to violate [break] the laws.'

He was reported to the Governor of Van Diemen's Land, who said, 'But you must know that you have broken the laws, or how came you here?'
    Loveless replied, 'By some means or other I was sent here; but I cannot see how a man can

break a law before he knows that such a law is in existence.'

This seems like common sense, but George Loveless was wrong. In the eyes of the law, not knowing that something is unlawful is no defence. The way Magistrate Frampton got the Tolpuddle Martyrs convicted and transported to Australia was cruelly harsh and unfair – it was not justice – but it was legally correct.

George Loveless was put in a chain gang working on the roads. This was bad, very bad. The men were forced to work all day in the hot sun by overseers who enjoyed using the whip. At night they were crammed together into 'Belly Bots', box-like cells with no room to lie down.

Harsh punishments were dealt out by magistrates in Australia for the slightest reason. Here is part of an 1834 Weekly Statement of Offences and Punishment:

'Making frivolous and vexatious charge against his master – 3 months hard labour on a road gang.
Being seen with a quantity of potatoes,

strongly suspected to have been stolen – 12
months hard labour on a chain gang.
Out after hours – six months hard labour on
a chain gang.'

The first of these offences was surely a
desperate convict telling the magistrate about
the cruelty of his master, and getting
punishment instead of mercy. In the second, a
starving convict was punished for an unproven
suspicion, being *seen* with potatoes! In the last,
the convict was simply out too late. His master
did not like him!

It was as well for George Loveless that he
spent only a week working in irons on the
roads, for the chain gangs broke the strongest
spirit. Governor Arthur saw his obvious
sincerity and put him to work on the
government farm.

Here George was not chained, but conditions
were still harsh. At night, he said, there were:
'Eight men, with only five beds, so of course the
new comer must go without; and this was my
portion, until some of the older hands

unfortunately got into trouble, and I was entitled to a bed, having been longer on the farm than others.

'Our hut was none of the best: in fine weather we could lie in bed and view the stars, in foul weather feel the wind and rain; and this added greatly to increase those rheumatic pains which were first brought on by cold irons round the legs and hard lying; and which, in all probability, will be my companions until I reach the tomb.'

Governor Arthur kept a close eye on George Loveless. He was a special prisoner, what might now be called a political prisoner. He was being punished for his beliefs, not really for breaking the law. This had been made clear when Judge Baron Williams sentenced the Martyrs at their trial in Dorchester '…for the sake of example…'. Sometimes, to make an example, overseers treated the Martyrs more harshly than other convicts. This seems to be what made Mr Scott treat James Brine so badly.

But if James Brine was a leader of the Tolpuddle union, George Loveless was leader of the leaders. Governor Arthur tried to be as fair as he could, because he knew that he himself might be questioned about his treatment of Loveless.

Crime among the convicts was in truth very high. The desperate struggle to survive set one convict against another. George Loveless reported that, '...In more than one instance during my stay in Van Diemen's Land has it been known that men so wretched and weary of life have taken an axe and murdered their companions for the sole purpose, as they have declared, of being hung to end their present wretchedness.'

George Loveless came close to the lash himself. His job on the government farm was to look after the livestock, some of which roamed wild in the bush. Nine of his cattle were rounded up as strays, and he did not miss them for a day. The overseer marched him to the magistrate and accused him of neglect of duty.

George described his day's work to the magistrate.

'I rise in the morning at sunrise, or before, and take the sheep to the bush to feed; I then return to the farm and milk nine cows and suckle as many calves; I am requested to follow the sheep and not lose sight of them, for fear of dogs which often get among and worry [attack] them; I am ordered to search for the wild cattle to see that none of them are missing; I had just been weaning the lambs, and the ewes being very restless, I was afraid of leaving them; and this, Sir, was the reason the cattle were taken to the pound and I did not miss them.'

Even the magistrate agreed that George had far too much to do and was blameless! He sent him back to work.

'I thank you, Sir,' said George, who had gone to the magistrate expecting to get fifty lashes. Like James Brine, George Loveless was determined to survive, taking each day as it came. He stayed true to his beliefs in true justice and the equality of all people.

The Tolpuddle Martyrs were made strong by bonds of friendship and family. But, when their thoughts turned to the green fields of Dorset, they were desperately anxious about their loved-ones.

Their wives and children would be suffering. If farmers and landowners in England thought the Martyrs were troublemakers who deserved punishment, they might punish the families as well. James Brine's older brother Charles was the only wage earner left to feed their mother Catherine, three young sisters and a younger brother. The cottages of all the families were owned by farmers, and to feed themselves, the older children had to work for those same farmers.

Were they starving? Had they been thrown out of their homes?

Chapter 11

Protest

from home

Iɴ England the magistrates, led by James
Frampton, were doing everything they could to
attack the families of James Brine and his friends.

The magistrates would not let the Tolpuddle
parish council give the families any money to buy
food. Help from the parish is what 'parochial
relief' means in this letter from Frampton to Lord
Howick, who was in the government.

'... It is perfectly true that I, and the other
Justices acting with me, refused to allow any
parochial relief for the wives and families of
those convicts; and we gave as our reason for

so doing that we had ascertained [found out] from the gaoler that they had been supplied by their wives with more food than they could consume [eat] during the time they were in gaol…'

What a reason! Diana Standfield, wife of Thomas and mother of John, was told to expect no help for herself or her five remaining children. The magistrates were reported to have said to her: 'You shall suffer want. You shall have no mercy, because you ought to have known better than to have allowed such meetings to have been holden in your house.'

George Loveless's wife, Betsy, was even threatened with transportation! She said in a letter: 'I told them [the magistrates] I could not remain to see the children perish for want, I would rather go to service [be a household servant] and leave the children with them; they said if I did they would transport me for it…'

Betsy Loveless found more generosity amongst people nearly as poor as herself, with families of their own to support. Her letter continues: 'Sir, had it not been for kind friends, we must have perished for want; out of a little they gave us a little, for none of the labourers here have but seven shillings per week...'

Once more the magistrates were setting an example. These important people wanted to make labourers afraid to join unions. They also tried to make it seem that labourers would be better off without unions. James Frampton's letter to Lord Howick continues: 'The Justices have particularly recommended to [told] the farmers... that every encouragement should be given to those labourers who did not join the Union by increasing their wages and placing them in all the most profitable work, so that they may feel the advantage of their good conduct...'

Magistrate Frampton acted on the advice of Lord Melbourne, the Home Secretary, just as he did before ordering the arrest of the Tolpuddle labourers. Many letters passed between them. Melbourne warned Frampton that he must give parish help to members of legal unions when they were out of work. But the Tolpuddle

Friendly Society of Agricultural Labourers was an illegal union because of its secret oath.

The Tolpuddle union had taken money from its members for the very reason of giving it back in times of need. Refusing parish help was another way for Frampton to hurt the union. He explained it this way:

> 'Our object in doing this [refusing help] was to prove to the labourers that the leaders of the Unions had deceived them if they [the unions] did not support their families; and if they did maintain them to lessen the funds of the Union at the same time that it relieved the parish.'

So this heartlessness set an example, used up the union's money and saved parish taxes!

George Loveless had three children at home, James Loveless two, and James Hammett one. There were five remaining Standfield children, and, of course, four younger Brines. Magistrate Frampton did not care if fifteen innocent children starved.

Luckily, other people did. The trial of the labourers was reported in newspapers across the whole of England. The Tolpuddle men themselves knew little of what was going on. George Loveless wrote this to his wife from the convict ship. 'Be satisfied, my dear Betsy, on my account. Depend upon it, it will work together for good and we shall yet rejoice together. I hope you will pay particular attention to the morals and spiritual interests of the children. Don't send me any money to distress yourself. I shall do well, for He who is Lord of the winds and waves will be my support in life and death.'

Trade unionists rallied to the cause. There was a mass meeting in London to protest at the sentences given to the Tolpuddle men. A relief fund was set up, and a cabinetmaker called Mr Newman took the coach to Tolpuddle. He carried money to Betsy Loveless, who wrote:

'But Sir, on Tuesday last a Gentleman came from London to enquire into our circumstance [ask how we were], and relieved us; he gave us £2-3s each, all equal alike; had it not been for this I cannot tell what we should have done.'

James Frampton's spies told him about Mr Newman, and the magistrate knew at once that he was not an important person like himself. He described the benefactor to Lord Melbourne as 'a very well-dressed person tho' not a gentleman...'; in fact '...a very suspicious person'!

Newman arranged for Mr Bridle, who was a shopkeeper in a nearby village, to make regular payments to all the families. The 'London Dorchester Committee' was formed to collect money and to try to get pardons for the labourers. Even before James and his friends had arrived in Australia, demonstrations to set them free were being held in England. The newspapers were writing about them, and questions were being asked in Parliament.

At a huge protest in London, over 50,000 people met at Copenhagen Fields. A peaceful procession wound its way through the streets for eight hours to take a petition to the office of Lord Melbourne. He refused to accept it when brought like this, though he did take it later to the King.

A newly elected Member of Parliament from Devon became a champion of the transported labourers. Thomas Wakley was a surgeon who had learned about politics by fighting for much needed change in medicine. Now he spoke up for the Tolpuddle men in Parliament.

Only King William could pardon them, if he was advised to do so by the Home Secretary. Lord Melbourne might never have given in, but in 1835 he became Prime Minister, and Lord John Russell took over as Home Secretary.

Lord John Russell believed in what we now call 'human rights'. He was a champion of reform – the putting right of past wrongs. Here at last was a chance for the Tolpuddle Martyrs to get the justice they deserved.

Chapter 12

Pardons!

I N England, friends of the Martyrs made a new plea for mercy, but had help come too late?

The Tolpuddle men were sentenced because they swore illegal secret oaths of loyalty to their union. Gradually, supporters realized that there were other examples of secret oaths – ones made by rich and important people. The Freemasons had secret ceremonies and swore secret oaths, and some Members of Parliament were Freemasons. The Orange Lodges swore secret oaths too, and the Duke of Cumberland was their Grand Master. He was the King's brother, and he was guilty of the same offence!

This was the lever Lord John Russell, as Home Secretary, needed to persuade King William to pardon the Tolpuddle Martyrs.

Lord Russell wrote to Lord Melbourne that '…it appears that the Duke of Cumberland and Lord Wynford have been doing the same thing only with more cunning, and deserve at least a more severe punishment'.

The King's brother a convict in Australia for seven years? He was far too important a person! It was unthinkable.

The King granted pardons in June 1835.

There was still argument and haggling. The government did not want the Loveless brothers back in England, and made this a condition of their pardons. The Home Secretary sent the vicar of Tolpuddle to visit their wives, Betsy and Sarah. The vicar asked if they would like to go to Australia. Neither would agree unless their husband wished it, so letters were sent by the next ship.

On 14 March 1836, Lord John Russell told Parliament that full, free pardons had been granted by the King to all six Tolpuddle men.

Free pardons would allow them all to return home. Here are the wonderful, flowery words of George Loveless's pardon.

'Whereas G. Loveless was at the Lent Assizes 1834 holden for the County of Dorset tried and convicted of administering Unlawful Oaths and sentenced to be transported seven years for the same – We in consideration of some circumstances hereby presented to us are Graciously pleased to extend our Grace and Mercy unto him and to Grant him Our Free Pardon for his said crime provided his conduct has during his residence in our island of Van Diemen's Land been satisfactory to the Governor thereof. Our Will and Pleasure therefore is that you do take notice hereof. And for so doing this shall be your Warrant. Given at the Court of St. James's the tenth day of March 1836, in the sixth year of our reign. William R.'

George and Betsy would 'yet rejoice together', as he had promised! But not at once. There were further delays and confusion because of the four months' sea voyage needed to carry a letter or a pardon half-way across the world. James Brine and the Tolpuddle Martyrs had been set free in England, but they were still convicts in Australia.

The authorities in Australia told them nothing about the efforts of people in England to set them free, and continued to treat them harshly.

There were further adventures in store for James Brine! At the end of 1835, the conditional pardons arrived from England. James was moved from his place of work, without being told why. He was treated as badly as he had ever been.

'I was there [a town near the coast] put in prison,' he wrote, 'and two days and two nights I was locked in the dark cells, with twelve ounces of bread and half a pint of cold water in twenty four hours. On the third night I was chained to fifteen more prisoners, and we were all compelled to lie down together in the open yard until morning.'

Imagine his confusion and fear. One day he was working on the farm, the next he was dragged across the countryside and thrown into prison – and nobody would tell him why.

He was taken by steamboat to Newcastle, on the coast of Australia, and for the next two weeks sat in prison with others waiting to stand trial. He felt so wretched, thinking he was to be punished for another crime he knew nothing about!

It seemed he was right, for he says that then, 'I was chained to about twenty others, and placed on board the steam-boat bound for Norfolk Island, the worst and most terrible of all the penal settlements… where punishments the most inhuman and cruel are daily practised…'

This was like a nightmare, with no waking up. George Loveless called Norfolk Island a 'hell upon earth' from which nobody ever returned. Was this the end for James Brine?

Is it you, Elizabeth?

JAMES Brine was chained up on the steamboat bound for Norfolk Island. This penal settlement was just a dot in the vast Pacific Ocean, a volcano sticking out of the sea 1,500 kilometres from mainland Australia.

Norfolk Island was notorious amongst the convicts as being the worst possible place to go. 'For all that are sent thither,' George Loveless wrote, 'are sentenced for their natural lives; so that every hope is gone of ever obtaining deliverance [being set free], or of enjoying any other society, or seeing any other but their miserable companions in infamy, wretchedness, and woe. Thus they are left to drag on their miserable existence, until death ends their sufferings.'

This was where prisoners were sent to be forgotten! Would James never return to the green rolling hills of Dorset? Would he never see his sweetheart Elizabeth again?

For once, luck was with James Brine, or perhaps his prayers were answered. The sea tried to destroy him, but instead delivered him from his enemies.

'After being some time at sea,' James wrote, 'a gale of wind sprung up which drove us back to Newcastle [the Australian port where they had started]. Being chained together on the deck, the waves kept continually dashing over us, and we were wet and miserable…'

Back on the mainland, James was glad for once to be thrown into prison. Anything was better than Norfolk Island!

After a while, James was reunited with Thomas and John Standfield, and James Loveless. They worked hard on farms for the rest of their time in Australia, although Thomas

Standfield became very ill because of the way he had been treated.

Then came a wonderful letter. Just when it seemed they could take no more, their prayers were answered!

George Loveless wrote to tell the others they were pardoned by the King. He had discovered they were free by reading about it in a newspaper: nobody had bothered to tell them!

Convicts who had served their time had to pay for their passage back to England. James had no money and he must have thought he would never get home. Then George explained how to claim a free place on a ship. Nobody else told James about this, either.

In New South Wales, James Brine danced for joy! He was going home! He and his three friends sailed aboard the *John Barry*, which made a long journey even longer by going by way of New Zealand. George Loveless sailed from Van Diemen's Land, alone as before.

Of the six Tolpuddle Martyrs, only James Hammett remained in prison. He was awaiting trial on a charge of assault. He must have been found guilty, for he did not leave Australia until another two years had passed.

The *John Barry* docked at Plymouth in Devon on Saturday 17 March 1838, and once more James Brine looked upon his homeland. Tears sprang to his eyes in the deliciously cool wind of that English spring.

Four years before, he had sailed from Plymouth as a convict bound for Australia. Now he stood on the Barbican Quay again, with a free pardon in his pocket. He had taken the worst that fate could throw at him, and he had survived!

Once more, James found himself tottering on land. After so many months at sea, the hustle and bustle of the port was almost too much to bear. Horse-drawn carts were rumbling across the cobbles. Dockworkers were loading boats with bales and barrels. People were hurrying to and fro, and everyone seemed to be shouting.

The first thing the friends wanted was a mug of ale at the Dolphin Inn on the Quay. There had been little cheer for them in Australia. When Mr Morgan the landlord found out who his customers were, the celebrations started!

James and his friends had been transported as villains. They returned in triumph as heroes. Plymouth townsfolk rushed down to the Quay. The Martyrs were invited to stay at the home of Mr Keast, who was a leading trade unionist in the building trade. Public meetings were held to welcome them home, in Plymouth, and then in Exeter.

James Brine had never spoken in public before. There were more people in each audience than lived in Tolpuddle! They had all come to hear a simple labourer tell his story.

James' hands sweated. His voice shook at first, but then grew strong as he told about the labourers' fight to get a decent wage, their trial and imprisonment in Dorchester Goal, the horror of the prison hulk at Portsmouth, the savagery of the convict ship on the high seas, the life of slavery in Australia and, at last, this joyful homecoming.

James Loveless and Thomas and John Standfield also told their stories. George Loveless's account was read aloud. Other people made rousing speeches, saying that all working people had been saved by the sacrifices of the Tolpuddle Martyrs. James felt proud and important.

Being a hero was very exciting, but what James really wanted was to see his mother and sisters again, and to hold dark-eyed Elizabeth in his arms.

They all wanted to be with their loved ones in Tolpuddle.

They had left Tolpuddle on foot with the constable, little suspecting what the future held. Now, they returned aboard a stagecoach carrying gifts that were heaped upon them. James hung his head out the window, straining for the first view of the village.

It was strangely unchanged. The same dusty street, the same low cottages, the creaking mill wheel, smoke rising from the smithy, the great sycamore spreading its canopy over the village green. These things seemed outside time, as if they would last for ever.

The stagecoach pulled up with a final lurch outside the Rose and Crown. The landlord threw open the door, calling, 'Welcome! Welcome home!'

As the weary travellers climbed stiffly down, men surged out of the Rose and Crown. Women and children ran out of the houses. All the families were there. Despite their hardships, none had lost their home.

James hugged his crying mother, his brothers and sisters. Every man in the village wanted to shake his hand. They slapped him on the back until he gasped for breath. All this time, his eyes were searching desperately. Where was Elizabeth?

'James! Don't you recognize me?'

Four years ago, Elizabeth had been a thin and awkward girl. Now she was a grown woman. Only her great dark eyes were the same. He would have to get to know her all over again!

Chapter 14

Enduring love

JAMES Brine was hardly more than a boy when he was transported to Australia. He was a young man of twenty-five when he returned. He had most of his life before him, and his adventures were not yet over.

It would have been very difficult for James and his friends to stay in Tolpuddle. Too many important people in Dorset hated them for having upset the old ways.

The London Dorchester Committee that fought for the Martyrs' release now asked for money from supporters all over the country, to help them settle in England. Enough was collected to rent farms in Essex.

The humble labourers were rising in the world!

James Brine shared New House Farm at Greensted Green with the Lovelesses. The Standfields took High Laver, about six kilometres away. Not far enough to keep James and Elizabeth apart!

On 20 June 1839, James and Elizabeth married at the little wooden church at Greensted. It was a great day, that united two people and the Brine, Standfield and Loveless families (Elizabeth's mother being a Loveless).

James was proud of his bride. He was proud, as well, that on the marriage certificate his job was recorded as 'farmer'.

The Tolpuddle Martyrs did not leave all their problems behind when they went to Essex. Some local people there thought they were troublemakers, and said so in public. The same vicar who married James and Elizabeth later protested in his sermons against 'convicts' being brought into his parish.

The Essex Morning Post said that the Martyrs 'diffuse a general sense of insecurity throughout that part of the country, and... disturb the habitual relation between the farmers and labourers...'. The newspaper printed a letter from a local magistrate that read, '...And lastly it is also true (and let me tell them they are marked men) that if these half dozen ignorant democrats (neither Essex men nor true agriculturalists are they) should attempt to disturb the peace of the county, they would be put down...'.

James and Elizabeth's first baby, Mary Jane, was born. George and Betsy Loveless had two more daughters. John Standfield married, and two sons were born to him and his wife.

The last of the transported men, James Hammett, returned from Australia. He stayed at New House Farm for a while and then he went back to Tolpuddle, where he lived for the rest of his days.

It was for the growing children that the Essex families decided to leave England and go to Canada, where they were not known.

The Brines and Lovelesses went first, in the spring of 1844. The Atlantic crossing was a cold and dangerous one. The ships were old and overloaded with emigrants, all hoping to start a new life in a land of opportunity.

James Brine's third daughter, Charity, was just a babe in Elizabeth's arms, but it was at George and Betsy Loveless's youngest child that tragedy struck. Sina died in mid-Atlantic, and her body was given to the waves.

All the families went to the Canadian state of Ontario, in the east of the country. James and Elizabeth Brine travelled by ox-cart, carrying a huge blunderbuss for protection. They rented a farm at Homesville, near Lake Huron. Disaster! A plague of grasshoppers ate James's crops!

The Brines moved nearer the town of London, where the Lovelesses had settled. The families helped each other. Eventually, James bought his own farm at St Mary's, close by. The log house he built himself became known as Brine's Corner. This farm prospered.

Each of the Tolpuddle Martyrs who emigrated to Canada did well in his own way. They kept their past a secret and were highly thought of by their neighbours. They did not want more trouble of the sort that had happened in England. Who can blame them?

James and Elizabeth Brine went on to have eleven children, none of whom knew of their father's adventures. When James died in 1902 at the good age of 89, the St Mary's Journal said that 'Mr Brine was highly respected. He was a man of sterling character and had the esteem of his fellow men in great measure.'

James and Elizabeth are buried side by side in St Mary's Cemetery, together in death as they were for their last half-century. Only James Hammett, of all the Martyrs, is buried in the village where he was born.

Their story reached Canada in 1912 with news of the building of a Memorial Arch at the Methodist chapel in Tolpuddle. In 1934, centenary celebrations were held in England and Canada.

Each summer, a festival of words and music is held in Dorset in their honour. Brine and Loveless descendants still meet to celebrate their ancestors. Working people and unionists still praise them. Without the Tolpuddle Martyrs, we would not have the prosperity and happiness that we enjoy today.

The Tolpuddle memorial, carved in white stone, reads: 'Erected in honour of the faithful and brave men of this village who in 1834 so nobly suffered transportation in the cause of liberty, justice and righteousness.'

These words are true, but they are not the whole truth. The greater truth is that it was for love of their families that the Tolpuddle Martyrs suffered so much. It was for the love that bound one family to another. It was for the enduring love between James and Elizabeth.

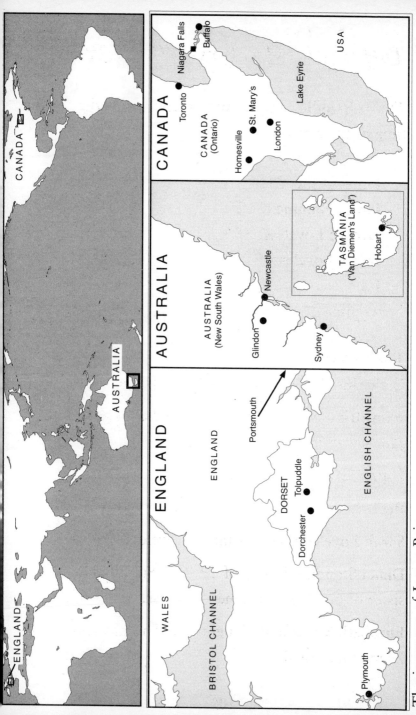

The journeys of James Brine.

Tolpuddle Martyrs' Who's Who

The Tolpuddle Martyrs with their ages at the time of their arrest

James Brine: 21
James Hammett: 22
George Loveless: 37
James Loveless: 25
John Standfield: 21
Thomas Standfield: 44

THE FAMILIES

Catherine Brine: mother of James Brine.

John Brine: father of James, who died when James was seventeen.

Harriet Hammett: wife of James Hammett.

Betsy Loveless: wife of George Loveless.

Sarah Loveless: wife of James Loveless.

Diana Standfield: wife of Thomas Standfield, sister of George and James Loveless.

Elizabeth Standfield: daughter of Thomas and Diana Standfield.

George Arthur: Lieutenant-Governor of Van Diemen's Land.

Mr Bridle: shopkeeper in Bere Regis who passed on money to the families.

Duke of Cumberland: Grand Master of the Orange Lodges and King William's brother.

James Frampton: chief magistrate in the Tolpuddle area.

Mary Frampton: sister of James Frampton.

James Keast: noted trade unionist living in Plymouth.

Edward Legg: one of the spies.

John Lock: one of the spies, James Frampton's gardener.

Lord Melbourne: Home Secretary at the time of the arrest, trial and transportation.

Mr Newman: cabinetmaker who brought money from London to the Tolpuddle families.

Lord John Russell: Home Secretary at the time of the pardons.

Robert Scott: farmer and magistrate, James Brine's 'owner' in Australia.

Thomas Wakley: champion of the Martyrs in Parliament.

William IV: King of England from 1830 to 1837.

Judge Baron John Williams: judge at the trial of the Martyrs.

Charles Woolaston: half-brother to James Frampton, and Dorchester magistrate.

Time Line for James Brine

1813	James Brine born
1830	Swing riots
1832	Meetings between Tolpuddle landowners and labourers
October 1833	Labourers' union formed
9 December 1833	Spies at meeting
24 February 1834	Martyrs arrested
19 March 1834	Sentenced to transportation
21 April, 1834	Demonstration at Copenhagen Fields
11 April – 25 May 1834	Convict ships leave England
17 August – 4 Sept 1834	Convict ships arrive Australia
April 1835	Lord John Russell becomes Home Secretary
June 1835	Conditional pardons granted
10 March 1836	Full pardons granted
30 January 1837	George Loveless leaves Australia

13 June 1837	George Loveless arrives home in England
11 Sept 1837	James Brine, James Loveless, and the Standfields leave Australia
17 March 1838	Brine, Loveless & Standfields arrive in England
August 1838	The move to the Essex farms
8 March 1839	James Hammett leaves Australia
20 June 1839	James Brine and Elizabeth Standfield marry
August 1839	James Hammett arrives home in England
29 December 1840	Birth of James and Elizabeth's first child, Mary Jane
Spring 1844	The Brine and Loveless families move to Canada
Spring 1846	The Standfield family moves to Canada
11 April 1902	James Brine dies

Source material

A note about illustrations

Photography had not been invented in the early nineteenth century, and only rich people could afford to have their portraits painted. So there are no reliable likenesses of James Brine and his friends when they were young.

With younger readers in mind

The Tolpuddle Martyrs: the Story of the Martyrs told through Contemporary Accounts, Letters and Documents, London: TUC Publications, 2000.

A lively, magazine-style version of the story.

The Tolpuddle Martyrs, Interactive CD ROM, London: TUC Publications, 2000.

The bare bones of the story narrated by the TV actor Tony Robinson.

With older readers and adults in mind

Laurie Lee, *Cider with Rosie,* London : Hogarth Press, 1959.

This famous autobiography shows what life was like for children in the countryside before modern times. Enjoyable and easy to read.

Joyce Marlow, *The Tolpuddle Martyrs*, London: Andre Deutsch, 1971.

This fine book is packed with information, some of which cannot be found anywhere else.

Walter Citrine ed, *The Martyrs of Tolpuddle*, London: TUC Publications, 1934.

This book was published as part of the centenary celebrations. Many later books use the original documents found here.

The Story of the Tolpuddle Martyrs, and TUC Guide to the Old Crown Court in Dorchester, and Tolpuddle Village, London: TUC Publications, 1991.

A handy summary of events, people and places.

Tolpuddle: An Historical Account through the Eyes of George Loveless, London: TUC Publications, 1997.

The story told in documents of the time, largely from George Loveless's point of view.

Audrey Wirdnam, *Pidela: An Account of the Village of Tolpuddle, Dorset, from Early Times*, Tolpuddle: Beechcote Press, 1989.

A historical account of Tolpuddle village.

Original sources

George Loveless, *The Victims of Whiggery; being a statement of the persecutions experienced by the Dorchester Labourers; their trial, banishment etc. Also reflections upon the present system of transportation. With an account of Van Dieman's Land, its customs, produce, and inhabitants, dedicated (without permission) to Lords Melbourne, Grey, Russell, Brougham and Judge Williams*, Cleave Publishers: London, 1837.

George Loveless's words in *Tolpuddle Boy* are from this paper, written after he returned from Australia. It can be found in the British Library, and the TUC Libraries Collection at the University of North London.

James Loveless (and James Brine, Thomas and John Standfield), *A Narrative of the Sufferings of James Loveless, James Brine and Thomas and John Standfield. Four of the Dorchester Labourers. Displaying the Horrors of Transportation. Written by Themselves. With a Brief Description of New South Wales by George Loveless*, Cleave Publishers: London, 1838.

The words of James Brine, John Standfield and James Loveless in *Tolpuddle Boy* are from this paper, written after they returned from Australia. It can also can be found in the British Library, and the TUC Libraries Collection at the University of North London.

Local information

In **Tolpuddle, England** you can see where James Brine's adventures started. Thomas Standfield's cottage, where the oath was given, still exists. Next to it is the old chapel where George and James Loveless preached. The sycamore tree under which the labourers met still stands on the village green. James Hammett lies in the graveyard of the Church of St. John the Evangelist. The Martyrs Museum and Cottages for retired agricultural labourers were built as part of the 1934 centenary celebrations.

The Martyrs Museum welcomes visitors with a gift shop selling many of the publications listed on pages 114-115, and an exhibition. Books and memorabilia can also be bought by post:

The Tolpuddle Martyrs Museum, Tolpuddle, Dorchester, Dorset DT2 7EH,
telephone +44 (0) 1305 848237,
internet: www.tolpuddlemartyrs.org.uk

The Tolpuddle Martyrs Festival is held in Dorset in July each year, with speakers, music, workshops, exhibitions and theatre.

For information contact:

South West TUC, Church House,
Church Road, Filton, Bristol BS34 7BD,
telephone +44 (0) 117 9470521,
email: southwest@tuc.org.uk

In **Canada** you can see an impressive plaque to the Tolpuddle Martyrs at Siloam Cemetery in London, Ontario, and the Labor Memorial Park on Queen's Avenue in London is dedicated to them. James Loveless is buried in Mount Pleasant Cemetery in London, while George and Betsy Loveless, and Thomas and Diana Standfield, lie side by side in Siloam Cemetery. James Brine's timber home in Blanshard Township, St. Mary's, near London, still stands. The graves of James and Elizabeth Brine and many of their descendants are in St. Mary's Cemetery, where a sycamore tree to mirror the one in Tolpuddle was planted in 1992. James Brine's Canadian descendants have visited England to see for themselves the places that shaped his life. They hold family reunion picnics in Canada, and are justly proud of their famous ancestor.

In **Australia** convict records can be consulted at the Archives Authority of New South Wales and at the Archives Office of Tasmania, in Hobart. You can search a computer database for your settler or convict ancestors at some Australian museums. The stone cottage in which George Loveless lived on the Strathayr Estate near Richmond, Tasmania still exists. It was there that he learned of his free pardon, by chance, while reading a newspaper.

The Song of Freedom

Glossary

Blunderbuss a short musket that fires a big shot.

Bush wild countryside in Australia.

Bushranger an outlaw who roams the bush.

Ceremony things done in a very solemn way.

Colony a gathering of people living in a country new to them.

Combination see Trade Union.

Condemn to find someone guilty or to punish them.

Condition to do something only if something else is also done.

Convict someone found guilty of breaking the law, to find someone guilty.

Council people in charge of a small part of the country (a parish).

Court a place where a person accused of breaking the law is tried.

Democracy a government where everyone has equal rights.

Demonstration a gathering of many people showing how they feel.

Emigrant	Someone who leaves [emigrates] from their own country to live somewhere else.
Employer	someone who has other people working for them.
Felony	a serious crime.
Flog	to whip long and hard.
Friendly Society	see Trade Union.
Game	wild animals such as rabbits, pheasants and deer, killed for food.
Gentry/ gentleman	those thought to be better than ordinary people.
Government	the people in charge of a country.
Governor	the top person in charge of a colony.
Home Secretary	the person in charge of law and order in England.
Initiation	a ceremony for new members of a society.
Inherit	to be given something when the owner dies.
Jury	people who decide whether or not someone is guilty in a trial.
Just	fair and right according to the law, or to commonsense.

Justice	fairness. A judge or a magistrate can also be called a justice.
Martyr	someone who dies or suffers greatly for their beliefs.
Minister	one of the people in charge of a country.
Member of Parliament (MP)	someone chosen to represent a district, and the people who live there, in Parliament.
New South Wales	part of south-eastern mainland Australia.
Pardon	to forgive, a notice saying that someone is forgiven.
Parish	a small part of the country with its own church.
Parliament	the place where government is based.
Penal settlement	a place for the punishment of convicts.
Petition	to ask for something in writing, often with many people signing it.
Politics	to do with government.
Procession	people going somewhere in a line.
Protest	to argue strongly against something.

Rally	a gathering of people, supporting or opposing something.
Relief fund	help, money given to help someone.
Republic	a government with no king or queen.
Sentence	the punishment given someone found guilty of breaking the law.
Surgeon	a person trained to cure illness by cutting the body.
Trade Union/ Society	workers who group together to bargain with employers.
Transportation	taking convicts overseas for punishment.
Trial	a hearing in court to decide if someone is guilty of breaking the law.
Tyrant	an all-powerful ruler, the opposite of democracy.
Van Diemen's Land	the large island off the south-eastern tip of Australia, now called Tasmania.
Vigilance	the greatest care and attention.

Index

Alan Brown writes texts for picture books, story books for young children and novels for teenagers. His work is published at home and abroad, and is translated into a number of languages. *Tolpuddle Boy* is his second title in Hodder Children's Books' narrative non-fiction series, where he combines his fiction writing skills with his experience of teaching non-fiction subjects.

Alan Brown is fascinated by the way ordinary people, such as James Brine and the Tolpuddle Martyrs, do extraordinary things that change the world.

If you enjoyed *Tolpuddle Boy* you might like to read Alan Brown's earlier book, *The Smallpox Slayer*, about Edward Jenner – who deliberately infects a boy with smallpox. But Jenner wants to save lives, not destroy them. It's 1796, and smallpox kills one in four children. Jenner plans to end its reign of terror through a strange new process he calls vaccination. To do this, Jenner must fight ignorance and fear as well as the killer virus.